CANAL & CRUISING

The IWA Manual

Sheila Davenport

Photographs by Una-Jane Winfield

Fernhurst Books

Produced in collaboration with
The Inland Waterways Association

Published by Fernhurst Books
Duke's Path, High Street
Arundel, W. Sussex BN18 9AJ

British Library Cataloguing in Publication Data
Davenport, Sheila
   Canal & river cruising: the IWA manual.
   1. Great Britain. Inland waterways. Cruising
   I. Title II. Inland Waterways Association
   797.1

ISBN 1 898660 45 X

Acknowledgements

Fernhurst Books would like to thank Hoseasons Holidays and Calcutt Boats for providing the narrowboats *Wild Tansy* for the photo sessions on the Oxford Canal and Grand Union Canal, and Wessex Narrowboats for providing the narrowboat *Protector* for photo sessions on the Kennet & Avon Canal. Thanks also to Jim Wallace and Wally Head for crewing *Protector*.

The river photographs were taken using the cruiser *Solitude* on the River Thames. The publishers would like to thank her owners Cyril Bampton and Heather Galpin, and Chloé and Simon Davison for crewing.

Photographs

All photographs by Una-Jane Winfield except the following:
Harry Arnold: pages 4, 9, 10, 36, 44, 45.
Sheila Davenport: pages 5, 32 (left), 41.
Debbie McGhie: page 34, 42
John Woodward: pages 18 (left), 21 (top), 26–7, 28–9, 32 (right), 35.

Edited & designed by John Woodward
Artwork by Roy Davenport
Typeset by PPC Limited, Leatherhead
Printed in China through World Print

www.fernhurstbooks.co.uk

CONTENTS

THE CANAL AGE	4
WHERE ARE THE WATERWAYS?	6
BROAD AND NARROW CANALS	8
GETTING AFLOAT	10
WHAT TO TAKE WITH YOU	13
WHAT ABOUT THE CHILDREN?	14
ESSENTIALS	15
REGULAR CHECKS	18
GETTING UNDERWAY	19
STEERING, STOPPING AND TURNING	20
BOATING WITHIN THE RULES	22
MOORING	24
LOCKS	26
MANNED LOCKS	30
BRIDGES	31
MOVABLE BRIDGES	32
TUNNELS	33
OTHER PROBLEMS	34
BUYING YOUR OWN BOAT	36
ENGINES	38
FITTING OUT	39
LICENCES AND MOORINGS	40
LOOK ABOUT YOU	42
FURTHER INFORMATION	46
GLOSSARY	48

THE CANAL AGE

It is difficult to believe that the tranquil scene pictured here was the starting point for some 150 years of hectic engineering and commercial activity. This is Worsley on the Bridgewater Canal, which was opened in 1761. Although it was not the first British man-made waterway, the Bridgewater Canal marked the beginning of the great age of canal building in Britain. The canals were made necessary by the Industrial Revolution, for although rivers had always been used for transport between the towns along their banks, the new manufacturing centres were developing in mineral-rich areas that were often some distance from rivers. The existing roads were often impassable in bad weather and quite inadequate for the needs of the new factories.

So the Canal Age began. All over the country speculators formed companies to raise funds to build canals, often without taking proper account of the problems involved or checking whether the waterway would ever make a profit. Nevertheless money was invested, successful canals were built and engineering knowledge improved. By 1850 there were more than 4000 miles of navigable waterways crossing England and Wales, Scotland and Ireland.

Canal building was a labour-intensive business. Large gangs of navvies worked all over the country, earning a reputation for drunkenness and riotous behaviour, but performing engineering miracles with the simplest of tools. There were no excavators and dumper trucks then, just shovels and wheelbarrows!

➡ **Where it all started: Worsley Basin, on the Bridgewater Canal, from a Victorian postcard.**

Worsley Old Boathouse.

After the navvies had finished, the boats and boatmen arrived, often with their wives and families living and working alongside them on the boats. The life was a hard one, with long hours worked in all weather conditions by all the family; continually on the move, the children were rarely able to go to school.

Although canal transport was far more efficient than anything that had gone before, it eventually succumbed to competition from rail transport and an improved road system. Poor management by the canal companies had made matters worse, and by the early twentieth century the amount of freight carried by water had been drastically reduced. Despite attempts at

➤ **Dereliction and decay: the disused Basingstoke Canal in the 1960s. This stretch has now been restored.**

revival, narrowboat carrying proved to be a dying trade and in 1947 the companies which had not already sold out to the railways were nationalised. In 1962 the British Waterways Board was set up, but by this time many canals were impassable and there was very little commercial traffic. After the hard winter of 1962–3, when canals were frozen and the boats were at standstill, the BWB decided to stop narrowboat carrying. This decision really meant the end of a way of life which had lasted for 200 years, and most of Britain's waterways became disused and derelict.

Sadly neglected though they were, the waterways held a fascination for those who explored them, either on foot or by water, and in 1946 a small group of dedicated people banded together to do something to protect and improve what remained of Britain's most hidden asset. They formed the Inland Waterways Association, and began the campaign for the rehabilitation of the waterways. Although hundreds of miles had been lost, the new 'navvies' in the shape of volunteer working parties got to work and, year by year, managed to open up long stretches of the once derelict system.

If you cruise on the River Avon, the Stratford Canal or the Cheshire Ring, to name only three sections of the vast canal network, you ought to know that waterways such as these have been restored by the hard work of hundreds of volunteers, both working on the canals themselves and helping to raise funds.

Today the work continues. The IWA's Waterway Recovery Group works on waterways all over the country, co-ordinating restoration schemes, organising work camps and encouraging volunteers to carry out work in a professional manner. Restoration tasks include rebuilding lock chambers, making lock gates, dredging silted-up channels and clearing overgrown towpaths. The results not only benefit the canal-cruising fraternity; they improve the environment for everyone.

Start in Surrey and you can travel by boat all the way to Yorkshire; from the Wash you can navigate across England to Wales. There are over 3000 miles of connecting canals and rivers in England and Wales, and restoration projects are gradually extending this. Scotland's Caledonian and Crinan canals are popular cruising waters and Ireland has its own Grand Canal.

From London, the Grand Union Canal takes you to Birmingham, either starting from its junction with the Thames at Brentford or from Limehouse Basin in Docklands. From Birmingham, canals radiate in all directions – Liverpool, Manchester, Llangollen, Oxford, Northampton and Nottingham are all linked to Birmingham by water. From Liverpool you can cruise high across the Yorkshire Dales, a glorious journey that eventually brings you down to earth (and Leeds) via the great staircase of locks at Bingley. Going south from Yorkshire the River Trent is tidal to Torksey, where you can make a detour from the Trent onto the Fossdyke and Witham Navigation. This is well worthwhile as Brayford Pool in Lincoln provides good moorings. Beyond Lincoln, the Witham takes you to Boston and the Wash.

The Middle Level and Fenland Navigations connect with the main systems by way of the River Nene, and these not so well-known waters have a charm of their own, with Cambridge and Ely offering plenty of interest for the visitor.

The River Thames is the south of England's most popular waterway, giving access to the River Wey Navigation – a delightful rural route from Weybridge to Godalming, which in its turn connects with the Basingstoke Canal. After many years of hard work by volunteers, this waterway is once again navigable. Also connecting with the Thames, the once-derelict Kennet and Avon Canal (entered under an uninspiring railway bridge just below Reading) has also been restored and the re-opened canal one again provides an east-west link from London through to Bristol.

You can leave the Thames at Brentford, four miles below Teddington, to join the Regents Canal (now part of the Grand Union) which takes you through London past the Zoo and finally links, via the short Hertford Union Canal or the Limehouse cut, with the Lee and Stort Navigation. It's a long way from the main system, but once past the suburban areas it develops into a very pleasant route passing through the Lee Valley Regional Park before dividing into two routes: one going to Bishops Stortford and the other to Hertford.

Three other routes in the south-east deserve a mention. The River Medway, reached via the Lower (tidal) Thames, is tidal to Allington. Careful navigation is needed here as you are likely to meet much larger craft along the route. From Allington, some 18 miles and nine locks take you through the Kentish countryside to Tonbridge. Further north in Essex, the Chelmer and Blackwater Navigation goes from Chelmsford to join the sea at Heybridge Basin. Only 14 miles long and restricted to boats of less than 2ft 6in draft, it is nevertheless a delightful waterway and well worth visiting.

In the Middle Ages, excavations for peat scarred the flat Norfolk landscape just as gravel workings crater the countryside today. Subsequent flooding of these 'peat mines' resulted in the lakes known today as the Norfolk Broads. The rivers and dykes connecting the Broads give around 120 miles of lock-free boating. There is no connection to the main canal system, but the area has been popular with holidaymakers for many years, with hire companies of over 50 years' standing offering both motor and sailing cruisers.

The network of canals and river navigations covers much of the country, and wherever you go you will view the countryside – and the towns – from an entirely new angle. It is impossible to describe adequately the fascination of exploring these remote waterways – go and see for yourself.

THE PRINCIPAL INLAND WATERWAYS OF ENGLAND AND WALES

Miles

10 0 10 20 30 40 50 60

10 0 10 20 30 40 50 60 70 80 90

Kilometres

KEY

— **Broad waterways**
(Locks over 7 ft. wide)

— Narrow waterways

- - - **Not completely navigable**
but subject to a restoration
project or proposal

There are far more
restoration schemes
planned, or in progress,
than can be shown on
the map. For details of
the current restoration
work contact the Inland
Waterways Association

NORTH SEA

THE WASH

CHANNEL

Tewitfield
LANCASTER
Lancaster
RIPON
Ripon
R.Ure R.Ouse R.Foss
YORK
R.Wharfe
Driffield
Beverley Beck
R.Hull
KINGSTON-UPON-HULL
PRESTON
BURNLEY
Leeds and Liverpool
LEEDS
R.Aire
Aire and Calder
Selby
R.Ouse
R.Derwent
Pocklington
R.Humber
Rufford
Calder and Hebble
R.Don
R.Ancholme
Leigh Branch
LIVERPOOL
MANCHESTER
Rochdale
Huddersfield
Narrow
Broad
Ashton
Peak Forest
Stainforth and Keadby
R.Idle
GAINSBOROUGH
Manchester Ship
Bridgewater
SHEFFIELD
Sheffield & S.Yorks
R.Trent
R.Mersey
R.Weaver
Macclesfield
Chesterfield
RETFORD
Fossdyke
R.Witham
Witham Navigable Drains
Shropshire
Whaley Bridge
CHESTERFIELD
WORKSOP
BOSTON
R.Dee
Caldon
LEEK
STOKE-ON-TRENT
Cromford
Erewash
Sleaford
Kyme Eau
Llangollen
Union
Middlewich Branch
Trent and Mersey
DERBY
R.Trent
NOTTINGHAM
Grantham
Grantham
Newtown
Montgomery
Caldon
Burton-upon-Trent
Leicester Section
Grand Union
R.Glen
KINGS LYNN
Norfolk and Suffolk Broads
NORWICH
Birmingham Canal Navigations
Coventry
Ashby
Oxford
Market Harborough Arm
R.Nene
R.Welland
PETERBOROUGH
R.Wissey
R.Little Ouse
R.Lark
LOWESTOFT
Stourport-on-Severn
Droitwich
B'ham & Fazeley
Welford Arm
Middle Level Navigations
R.Cam
R.Gt.Ouse
WORCESTER
Worcs & Birm
Stratford
COVENTRY
Grand Union
NORTHAMPTON
R.Nene
CAMBRIDGE
R.Avon
STRATFORD-ON-AVON
Northampton Arm
R.Gt.Ouse
Upper
BEDFORD
Sudbury
R.Stour
Evesham
TEWKESBURY
Lower
Chelmer and Blackwater
GLOUCESTER
Gloucester & Sharpness
Aylesbury Arm
HERTFORD
BISHOPS STORTFORD
Chelmsford
Stroudwater
Thames and Severn
R.Thames
OXFORD
Grand Union
R.Stort
R.Lee
R Crouch
Brecon & Abergavenny
Paddington Arm
Regents
R.Thames
R Roach
Pontypool
R.Severn
Slough Arm
LONDON
BATH
Avon
Kennet and Avon
R.Kennet
READING
Grand Union
R.Medway
MAIDSTONE
BRISTOL
Basingstoke
GUILDFORD
TONBRIDGE
R.Wey
Godalming
Wey and Arun
BRIDGWATER
Bridgwater and Taunton
TAUNTON
Winchester
R.Parrett

Because there was no overall plan when the canal system came into being the network is a curious mixture of broad and narrow canals.

'Broad' canals have locks that are over seven feet wide (usually 14 feet) and 'narrow' canals have locks with a maximum width of seven feet. This means that if you want to explore the entire canal system you cannot use a boat with a width (beam) of more than seven feet, and 6ft 10in is really the practical maximum.

On broad canals the locks have double gates at both ends and the whole process of passing through a lock takes a little longer. Narrow canals usually have two bottom gates and one top gate; your boat is easier to handle as it slots into the lock neatly and cannot swing about in the lock chamber as the water comes in. But just before you rush off to plan your next holiday on a narrow canal, it might be worth mentioning that some of the longest flights of locks are on narrow canals! Tardebigge on the Worcester and Birmingham Canal has 30 locks and there are 27 locks on the stretch leading into Wolverhampton. But even these are light work compared to Hatton Locks near Warwick on the Grand Union Canal – a flight of 21 closely-spaced broad locks climbing round a hill – or the 23 broad locks at Wigan on the Leeds and Liverpool Canal.

The terms 'broad' and 'narrow' refer to the dimensions of the locks, rather than to the actual channel. This may be anything from 14 feet to 40 feet wide, although there will be sections where bank erosion, encroaching weed or shallow water will reduce the usable width of the canal.

◆ A narrow lock on the Oxford Canal. The lock chamber is just wide enough to accommodate a traditional narrowboat with a seven-foot beam.

◆ Stockton Locks on the Grand Union are broad locks, able to accommodate two narrowboats abreast. Boats with a broader beam can also use this canal, but they cannot penetrate the stretches of 'narrow' canal that link it to other parts of the waterway network.

TIDAL WATERS

This book is mainly concerned with non-tidal waters: either man-made canals where the flow is non-existent; or navigable rivers that are controlled by locks and weirs. These river navigations allow a considerable flow of water (particularly after heavy rain) but are totally unlike their tidal lower reaches. You will find these tidal sections referred to in navigation guides as 'tidal below' certain points. At these points the newcomer to cruising should turn round and go back.

There are various reasons for this. In the first place hire companies do not normally allow their boats on tidal waters. Your boat also needs to be of a suitable type and equipped with items that you wouldn't use on sheltered inland waters – such as very long ropes and anchors – plus an engine of sufficient power to enable you to make headway against a fast-flowing tide. You also need to be able to work out tidal rise and fall if you are to avoid being stranded, and be experienced enough to handle the boat in a current.

So the point here is that navigation on tidal waters is not for beginners. The time will come when you will want to explore routes with tidal sections, and then you must find out all you can beforehand by writing to navigation authorities for information, checking tide tables, consulting lock keepers and enquiring at local boat clubs. But newcomers to cruising should be patient, improve their boating skills and stay well clear of tidal waters.

You can explore inland waterways on almost any type of boat. You can use a rowing boat or a canoe for a day trip (take a tent for a longer outing), a small cruiser or a narrowboat for a few days, or book yourself into a hotel boat for a week.

Should you buy or hire? Whatever you do, *don't* rush out and buy a narrowboat the moment you discover inland waterways! Do hire a few boats before you consider buying; you will get some idea of the sort of boat you would like, you'll have the opportunity to talk to boat owners you meet on the water – and most importantly you will find out just how much you like cruising.

Hiring

There are hire firms operating on most of the canals, rivers and Broads, all offering boats ranging from two/four berth up to 12 berth – although some companies restrict their larger boats to experienced hirers. Charges vary according to the type of boat, for they range from extremely luxurious craft to basic camping boats. The latter are often ex-working narrowboats, and can provide excellent opportunities for youth groups and school parties to get afloat.

The cost also varies according to the time of year, reaching a peak in August. The holiday 'season' used to run from late March to mid September, but it is being extended as more and more companies offer off-peak holidays at cheaper rates. Christmas on a canal can make quite a change! The boats come equipped with every 'mod. con.' so you'll be warm inside the boat whatever the weather, but many spring and autumn days can be as fine as summer ones, so it's worth considering off-peak bookings.

➥ **If you find a narrowboat too constricting, you could try spreading yourself on a Broads cruiser.**

As well as some form of heating, you can expect to find a full-sized cooker, a refrigerator, hot water and a shower, plus optional hire of a television set. You may have to pay extra for bed linen, towels and tea towels, or you may choose to bring your own. Some companies do not allow dogs on board; others will, but may make a small charge.

In most cases you will have to return the boat to its starting point, so make allowance for this when you are planning your route, and don't be over-ambitious! A late return to the boatyard may incur a hefty surcharge, as it could upset the yard's turn-round schedule.

Learning the ropes

Before you leave on your holiday, you will need some tuition. Someone from the boatyard should take you out in the boat and explain the mechanics, give you some instruction in boat handling and show you how to moor and work locks. Do ask about this when you book, and don't hesitate to ask questions on the spot. Every boat is different and each waterway has its own characteristics. It's in everyone's interest to see that you don't spoil your holiday – or the boat! Boat handling is largely a matter of common sense; it's not difficult, but first time round it takes a little getting used to.

Licences

All boats must be licensed for the waterways they are to be used on. Hire boats are licensed by the hire company, but you may want to use the boat on a waterway for which it is not licensed. If this is part of your plan, you should consult the company first.

Just a note about fishing. The boat is licensed for navigating, not angling! If you intend to use your fishing tackle on the boat, the rules are the same as the rules for anglers sitting on the bank. Look out for angling club signs, purchase day tickets where needed and make sure you have a rod licence if required.

How far can I go in a week?

This is one of the most frequently-asked questions – and one of the hardest to answer! So much depends upon you and your crew. Do you want to visit towns and places of interest, or would you rather be on the water all day? Do you like to be up and about early, or do you feel that a holiday is for oversleeping? Have you got a crew of young people all eager to have a go at locks, or are there just two of you? All these things will determine how far you can travel, but you can begin to plan on the basis of a unit known as a 'lock-mile'.

If you remember that, on canals, your boat is not allowed to travel at more than four miles per hour, and if you allow a quarter of an hour for passing through each lock, then:

$$1 \text{ mile} = \tfrac{1}{4} \text{ hour} = 1 \text{ lock}$$

So for any journey, you add the locks to the miles and get an answer in 'lock miles'. Since you can do four lock miles an hour, you can work out how long your proposed trip will take. Cruising on canals for six hours each day means that you could do 24 lock miles a day – so a week's holiday will allow you to do up to 140 lock miles. This allows time for checking in at the boatyard, and getting the boat back on time. On river navigations you may be able to travel a little faster and you could average six lock miles an hour, so you may be able to travel further if your route involves a lot of river work.

These figures are intended as a guide only. You may feel you can work through locks more quickly, particularly where the locks are in flights, but it is impossible to maintain a speed of four miles per hour for long – three or even two miles per hour is a much more likely average figure.

With the continuing re-opening of once-derelict canals, 'rings' are being created such as the Cheshire ring, the Avon ring and the Warwickshire ring, and you'll see these advertised in hire company brochures. The advantage of these 'ring' cruises is that you don't cover the same ground twice; their disadvantage is that once you are past what you think is the half-way mark, you're stuck with getting back to the boatyard on time without knowing what lies ahead! Do take advice from the hire company on the timing of any ring cruise.

Stoppages

The canal system is, in places, over 200 years old. For various reasons there has rarely been sufficient money spent on maintenance: the original canal companies couldn't afford to, and during the years of decline the backlog of maintenance grew to enormous proportions. British Waterways, on a limited budget, have an annual work programme. The major repairs are normally carried out during the winter months, when there are fewer boats on the move, so if you are thinking about cruising in winter, contact British Waterways and ask for a stoppage programme.

This details the main closures, but from time to time sections of the system are closed at short notice to deal with unexpected problems. It you are hiring, your boatyard will be aware of any problems and advise you of alternative routes. If you are cruising in your own boat you can make sure that there are no emergency stoppages affecting your route by ringing 'Canalphone', the British Waterways information line. There are two numbers: one for the north and one for the south. Details of the dividing line and the numbers are available from British Waterways.

When the sun is blazing down and it seems to be ideal boating weather, the canal system tends to suffer from water shortage problems. It is rare to encounter a full-scale closure owing to water shortage, but you may find areas where the use of locks is restricted, usually by flights of locks being closed at around 4pm. 'Closed' normally means padlocked – so don't think you can sneak through when no-one is looking! If you find you're boating during a prolonged heatwave, check before you go and plan accordingly.

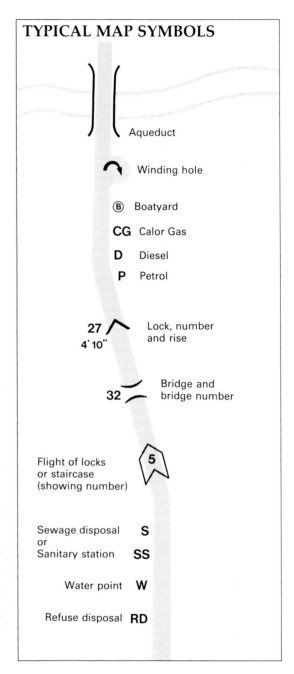

TYPICAL MAP SYMBOLS

Aqueduct

Winding hole

Ⓑ Boatyard

CG Calor Gas

D Diesel

P Petrol

27
4' 10"   Lock, number and rise

32   Bridge and bridge number

Flight of locks or staircase (showing number)   5

Sewage disposal **S**
or
Sanitary station **SS**

Water point **W**

Refuse disposal **RD**

Most people take far too much when they go on holiday. When you are embarking on a boating holiday, where storage space is limited, the packing list should be pruned ruthlessly.

As with any outdoor holiday, though, you need to be prepared for anything. Early morning starts and evening strolls along the towpath can be surprisingly chilly, so be sure to include warm sweaters. Boating wear should be comfortable and expendable – canal locks are ideal places for collecting grease and mud! You will need rubber- or rope-soled shoes to stop you slipping on deck and to avoid damaging the boat. You can buy yachting shoes from chandlery stores or use chain-store plimsolls or trainers; whichever you choose, check them before you go to make sure that the non-slip sole hasn't worn away to a smooth surface. Wellington boots are useful too, for towpaths can get very muddy after rain, but they are not ideal for wearing on board.

Wet weather is best dealt with by wearing a lightweight sailing suit. This will take up very little storage room, and when worn over a thick sweater it will keep you warm and dry.

Take a torch with you; you'll find it useful returning to your boat after dark. A first aid kit is essential – include all the usual things, and don't forget something for insect bites and stings, plus insect repellant if you're one of the unfortunates whom the gnats seek out! A pot of hand cream can be valuable for soothing rope-chafed hands; you might consider wearing gloves for rope handling.

Cameras and binoculars need to be in their cases, or else tucked away in plastic bags.

If you take your radio, do remember that your listening choice may not be everyone else's. Most people do not realise just how far sound travels along a quiet waterway, particularly at night.

◗ **Narrowboats are more comfortable than you might think, but there is little space to spare, and certainly no room for bulky suitcases. Pack everything in soft holdalls, rucksacks, or even black plastic bin liners.**

Cooking aboard

You can – or you needn't! The boat will be equipped with a sink, fridge, cooker, pans and utensils (usually fairly basic, so take your own favourite kitchen knife). You can cook as you would normally at home, although it's as well to remember that in warm weather the galley can get very hot: cooking a roast tends to cook the cook, too.

But wherever you go, you can probably plan to moor near a pub or within reach of a town where you can find somewhere to eat out, so it doesn't have to be a non-holiday for whoever normally cooks at home.

The children will enjoy being afloat; on the move there's always something to watch, and careful planning will enable you to visit swimming baths and places of interest along the route.

Older children will enjoy helping at locks, but should always be supervised. In most canals the water is not very deep *except at locks*, where the rise and fall can be 12 feet or more. Even if the children can swim, lifejackets and a watchful adult eye are essential at locks. Don't let children run around the lockside or climb across gates. Make sure they understand how locks work and don't leave a little 'un struggling with a paddle – it may hurt his pride to have you take over, but it would hurt even more if the windlass slipped.

If you are on a narrowboat there'll be room for a few favourite (small) toys. Plenty of paper and coloured pencils are a good standby, and a family board game helps on wet days. Babies still at the 'feed and sleep' stage can be dealt with as you would at home, but don't forget that although the baby is small, its luggage will take up a lot of room!

Toddlers are probably the most difficult to deal with, on or off boats. Things like cooker controls and cupboard doors are ideally placed for little fingers and you haven't got the garden for those desperate moments. This doesn't mean you have to abandon the idea of a boating holiday if you have toddlers, but you do need to allow plenty of time for going ashore and letting off steam. You also need enough crew members to ensure that someone is always available to look after the child.

➡ **Junior crew members will want to steer, but never leave a child to steer unsupervised, and don't hesitate to take over if an awkward situation arises. Insist that non-swimmers wear lifejackets whenever they are on the outside of a moving boat.**

BOAT SAFETY

● Hold on with one hand whenever you move about on deck.
● Make sure the children wear lifejackets in any situation when they might fall into the water.
● Wear non-slip rubber or rope-soled shoes on board.
● Insist that non-swimmers stay in the cockpit when the boat is moving.
● Make sure that everyone knows where the lifebelt is, and understands how to use it.
● Check that the lifebelt is ready for use.
● Check the contents of the first aid box, and be sure that everyone is familiar with the technique of artificial resuscitation.
● Never jump off the front of a moving boat; if you slip the boat may run into you and crush you.
● Do not try to stop the boat by fending off with your feet or hands – you will have little effect and you may be seriously injured.

ESSENTIALS

Gas

Your cooker will run on bottled gas. If you're hiring a boat you can be reasonably sure that there will be sufficient for your holiday. There will probably be two cylinders on board: one in use and one in reserve. The boatyard will explain how to change them over if one runs out. In your own boat, you'll be able to replace cylinders at canalside chandlery stores and boatyards.

Your cooker will operate in just the same way as a mains gas cooker. It will probably be self-igniting, but it is a good idea to add a box of matches to your stores list, just in case.

The main difference between 'boat' gas and 'domestic' gas is that you should always turn boat gas off at night, or if you are leaving the boat for some time. In exceptionally hot weather this may cause problems with the contents of the fridge, but normally the fridge will be cool enough to last through the night. Leaving a couple of previously-frozen ice packs in the fridge helps. If you do decide to leave the gas on, check that all pilot lights are still burning in the morning.

In the unlikely event of a leak the gas, being heavier than air, will collect in the bilges unheeded until there's sufficient to explode when someone starts the engine or lights a match. Hence the importance of turning it off at the cylinder. If you do suspect a leak, turn off the gas and the engine, don't let anyone smoke and contact your boatyard immediately.

Water

Water is kept in a storage tank on board. On all but the tiniest of boats this tank will be connected to a tap at the sink, where it is pumped out by hand or by electric pump. On a hired narrowboat you will find electric pumps, and you can expect to have both hot and cold water. The boat's water tank will be of a suitable capacity for the number of people aboard, but it will need replenishing from the water points which occur fairly frequently on most waterways.

Large cruisers and narrowboats will have a water filler point on deck, and will carry a hose to connect with the water point. There's also a filler cap for the fuel; they should both be clearly marked and well separated, but take care not to get them mixed up! On small boats where the tank may only be accessible from inboard, you will probably find it easier to fill it with a portable one- or two-gallon container; a funnel helps with this. Water points are shown in the navigation guides, and it's good practice to make a daily check on the water situation and the whereabouts of the next tap.

Rubbish

You must never throw your rubbish on to the bank or into the water. Quite apart from the awful visual impact of tins, bottles and old wrappings scattered along the canal bank, they can injure farm and wild animals, as well as children walking or playing on the towpath.

GAS SENSE

- Turn off the gas at the cylinder when it is not in use.
- Turn off the gas at night – and never sleep in the cabin with a gas heater burning.
- Ensure that the cabin and galley are well ventilated.
- Light the gas cooker as soon as you turn it on.
- If you have a gas oven, be careful to close the door gently or you may blow the gas flame out.
- Never leave the gas burning unattended.
- Check all burners and pilot lights regularly to make sure that they have not blown out.
- If you suspect a gas leak, turn off the gas at the cylinder, make sure no-one is smoking, leave the boat if possible and contact your boatyard immediately.

Please use bio-degradable washing-up liquid if you can get it. Many large supermarkets are now stocking these products. The effect of detergents on canal wildlife is greatly reduced if they break down quickly in the water.

You will find waste disposal points at locks, sanitary stations, boatyards and mooring sites; use them! Add a packet of black plastic sacks to your initial stores list, so that you can bag all rubbish. You may find that the dustbins at one particular site are full; if so, don't add to the heap unless you have to and are able to leave your rubbish properly bagged.

Toilets
All canal boats have chemical toilets of one sort or another. Sea toilets which discharge overboard are not allowed on inland waters. There are two basic types. Recirculating toilets hold the treated waste either in a large sealed tank on board or in a smaller portable tank incorporated in the toilet unit. Less popular, though eminently practical and simple to use, are the 'bucket and chuck it' variety – there's no pump to fail and they're very easy to clean.

If you've got a sealed holding tank on board you'll need to find a pump-out point to empty it. These can be found at most boatyards, but there is a charge for pumping out; hire companies may have reciprocal arrangements with others in their area, or may refund any charges you pay.

If you've got a portable unit, you should look out for the small brick or concrete buildings labelled 'sanitary stations'. Some of these are locked, so you need to make sure that you have a key. Your hire company will supply one, but if you're cruising in your own boat, the information that comes with your licence will tell you where to get a key. Disposal points are indicated in navigation guides and will usually have water taps and rubbish bins on the same site.

◆ **Emptying a chemical toilet with a portable tank is simplicity itself. Pulling out a lever unlocks the top section (far left) which can then be removed to reveal the holding tank below (centre left). This can be carried away like a suitcase (centre right) and emptied at a sanitary station (right). Never empty the tank into the canal, on the bank or down an ordinary drain.**

Fuel

Large hire boats with diesel engines are likely to carry ample fuel for several weeks' holiday. Petrol engines, particularly thirsty outboards, will need more attention and here you need to look at a map or guide to see where fuel can be obtained. Waterside filling stations or boatyards selling fuel can be hard to find on some canals. Owners of boats with outboard engines would do well to invest in a second fuel tank so there is always one in use and one in reserve; when one tank is empty you can take the first opportunity to fill up. Even this twin tank system can fail, though, and you may be faced with a walk to the nearest town or village – in which case a one-gallon can is an advantage.

When filling tanks or transferring petrol from one to another don't forget the usual safety precautions: don't smoke, turn all gas burners off and fill the outboard tanks on the bankside rather than on board, wiping off any spillage before you return them to the boat.

Breakdowns

If your own boat fails you'll probably have a fair idea of what's gone wrong. There are a few obvious checks to make, and your engine manual will include a 'troubleshooting' section. Check your engine daily: a well-maintained engine will give you very little trouble.

The situation is a little different on a hired boat. The operators take great care to see that their engines are well looked after, and they won't relish the thought of an amateur mechanic poking around! The first thing to do is make sure that you have done all the things on the daily check list. Then check the propeller is clear: weed, polythene bags or rope wrapped around it will all affect the performance in varying degrees. If it is a starting problem, have you turned everything on? Check the battery; did you use a lot of power the night before? Was it a wet evening with all lights on and the television going until the small hours?

Once you have established that you need help (and you nearly always will) then you'll need to contact the boatyard. It may be a long walk to the nearest phone, but you may be able to hitch a lift on the next passing boat. If you send someone else, make sure that he or she can explain exactly how the breakdown happened and what the situation is; non-starting, engine misfiring or whatever. And make sure that you know where you are – use bridge numbers or lock names for reference if you're out in the fields.

While on the subject of telephones and contact with the outside world, you have to remember that boating is about getting away from it all. This is fine – unless you have relatives or dependants who might be a bit doubtful about your being out of touch for a week or so. You will find the normal callbox in towns and villages, and probably at boatyards, but it's far better not to promise to ring someone *every* day or at a particular time. It will upset them – and you – if you can't make it.

➡ **Fuel, water and pump-out facilities for sealed toilets can be found at regular points along the canals, and their locations are indicated in the waterway guides.**

DIESEL ENGINES

♦ Use the bilge pump to clear water from the bilges. Do this as the boat is moving, when the stern is lower than the bows, so the water flows back to the pump inlet in the stern.

♦ Screw up the stern gland until you feel a resistance, then give it a full turn to squirt grease into the bearing. Do this each morning and evening.

♦ Check the engine oil at least each week, as you would in a car. Check the gearbox oil at the same time.

♦ Top up the header tank daily using clear water from the boat's supply.

♦ Check the fuel using a clean dipstick. A 53-foot narrowboat will use about a gallon an hour.

PETROL ENGINES

♦ Turn off the stopcock and remove the water filter. Clean it, replace it, then turn on the stopcock again.

♦ Check the gearbox oil with the dipstick, and top up if necessary.

♦ Check the engine oil with the engine dipstick and top up if necessary.

♦ Squirt some grease into the stern gland, as with the diesel installation. Use the bilge pump to clear water from the bilges.

♦ Dip the fuel tank if your boat is not equipped with a fuel gauge.

There are two schools of thought about boat breaksasts. Some people go for the complete British meal, sending delicious bacon smells wafting down the moorings; others prefer hunks of bread and marmalade eaten while steering through the early morning mists! Whichever style you adopt, you must allow time for the daily check of the boat's equipment, as detailed on the previous page.

Doing this check will take you no more than fifteen minutes at most, but make sure that you work through the list every day. Hire companies ask you to do this to ensure that the boat runs well during your holiday – it's not their fault if you forget something and are left waiting for an engineer to plod across a couple of fields to rescue you! You should also check that the toilet is empty and the water tank is full.

➡ **If you have to push off with the boathook, stand on the boat and hold the shaft under your armpit; this way the end cannot be pushed into your body.**

Having made sure that everything's OK, start the engine *before* you cast off – because however sure you are that your engine is a first-time starter, there's always a chance that you will be left drifting, powerless. When the engine is running smoothly, you can cast off, first making sure that everyone is on board and that you've picked up the mooring pins. You'll normally move off forwards, but if the water is shallow it's better to go stern first. If the water is weedy, check that the propeller is clear; you may have picked up some weed on the way in. If you think the bow (or stern) needs pushing out, this should be done by someone on the boat and with the boat hook – otherwise you'll end up with someone astride an ever-widening gap between boat and bank. Once under way, check that the fend-offs (on a cruiser) are lifted clear of the water, and that the ropes are all coiled ready for use and not left trailing in the water where they could foul the propeller.

STARTING A DIESEL

1 Make sure the gear lever is in neutral and the clutch is out (button out).
2 Move the lever forward to full throttle.
3 Turn the ignition key until the heater plug light comes on. Hold this for 25 sections if the engine is cold, or less if the engine is still warm.
4 Turn the key fully until the engine fires.
5 Return the lever to neutral and engage the clutch (button in).
6 Check the cooling water is circulating (unless the system is sealed).
7 Push the lever into forward gear, and go!
8 To stop the engine, pull the decompressor lever, turn off the key and push the decompressor back in.

Traditional-style narrowboats have tiller steering and most cruisers have wheel steering. One thing which is common to both – and a little disconcerting until you get used to it – is the fact that when you steer the boat it swings about its middle. If you turn the bows to the left, the stern will swing out to the right, and vice versa. When you are learning to steer, you'll find you progress in a zig-zag fashion through the water. Take it gently: don't try and overcompensate – just watch the bows and as soon as they start to wander use a touch on the wheel or tiller to set you straight. A steering wheel works in the same way as on a car: 'left hand down a bit' and you turn left. But a narrowboat tiller works the opposite way and this can be a bit confusing at first. Perhaps the easiest way to sort it out is to remember that, if the boat is going the wrong way, *push the tiller that way too*.

You should also remember that steering becomes more difficult at slow speeds, and in a cruiser with an outboard it's almost impossible to steer in neutral gear. This doesn't mean that you should rush through narrow bridges and into locks, but it does mean that you need to be sure the boat is going where you want before you slow right down and go into neutral.

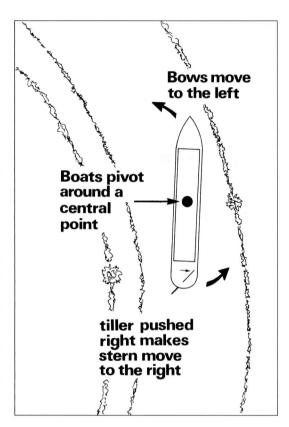

Bows move to the left

Boats pivot around a central point

tiller pushed right makes stern move to the right

➡ **Find the winding hole on the navigation chart or guide and motor up to it.**

➡ **Steer the bows of the boat into the winding hole (watch for shallow water near the bank).**

➡ **When the bows are close to the bank, shift into reverse and move the tiller over.**

◆ **Tiller steering can be confusing at first, and it helps to practise on an open stretch of canal before you have to perform a tricky manoeuvre at a lock or mooring.**

Very few boats handle well in reverse, and each has its own peculiarities when asked to retreat! The major use for your reverse gear will be to stop the boat. Perhaps it's stating the obvious to say that boats don't have brakes; you can't do the equivalent of an 'emergency stop'. Stopping a boat is a fairly lengthy procedure, so you must keep a good look-out at all times to ensure that you don't have to do anything in a hurry. Once a boat is moving, the only way to stop it is to put the engine into reverse, and it will be some time before the reverse drive stops the boat moving forward; the heavier the boat, the longer it takes. Experience will help here, as with all boat handling, but don't take chances. Approach all locks, bridges and doubtful situations very carefully.

You can't do a U-turn either! Unless you are on a small boat you'll need to find a wider-than-normal section of canal to turn round in. This may be at a junction or by a boatyard, but these aren't always ideal places as you may obstruct other boats. There are special turning places provided on canals; these are known as 'winding holes' and are marked on the navigation charts in guides.

or:

Having found a winding hole, go in bows first (watch out for shallow water close to the bank) and start to reverse out. It helps to give a sharp burst in reverse first, with the tiller hard over, and then let the boat swing round, with just a little help from the engine, using a combination of forward and reverse gears.

◆ **Allow the motor to pull the stern round. A short burst of power may help.**

◆ **As the stern swings round, the boat pivots on its centre and the bows swing out of the winding hole.**

◆ **When the bows are almost clear, shift into forward gear, push the tiller over, and go!**

Speed

The speed limit on canals is four miles an hour. this is a fast walking pace and is *the absolute maximum* – most of your cruising will be at three miles an hour, or less. Moored boats, shallow water or narrow sections of canal all mean that you have to slow down. Make a habit of glancing behind you to check on your wash – if you are making waves you are going too fast. Heavy wash damages banks, washes debris into the water and can cause considerable discomfort and even damage to moored craft. Slow down as you approach bridges and bends; keep a lookout for other boats, anglers and children in small boats, and reduce your speed accordingly.

This question of speed is fundamental. Canals were not built for motor boats; the original canal boats were horse-drawn. In fact, travelling with your engine roaring away will not have much effect, as the shallowness of most canals today slows the boat down. You'll be using an awful lot of fuel getting nowhere!

As far as river navigations go, the speed limit may be higher – but you must always navigate within the limits of safety, and with consideration for others.

➤ **Don't go too fast – check behind to make sure you are not making waves that will destroy the canal bank.**

Rules of the road

The first thing to remember is that the canal is *not* the road: you keep to the *right* (but not too close to the bank), pass other boats left side to left side and overtake to the *left* of other boats. The principles governing overtaking are the same as on the road: never on a bend or anywhere where you don't have a clear view of the water ahead, and never close to a lock or bridge.

It's good manners to slow right down and pull over if another boat wants to pass you. They are rarely in an awful rush; more commonly their engine's 'comfortable' speed is a little faster than yours. If you are wanting to overtake, wait until you can see that there is plenty of room to get by, particularly if it's a larger boat than yours. Quite often there is not enough deep water for them to pull over and let you by.

When you see another boat heading towards you, don't panic and head for the bank immediately – you are both travelling slowly and there is plenty of time to sort things out! Unless you are in an exceptionally narrow stretch there will be plenty of room for you to pass each other. Try to pass as close to the other boat as you feel able to – a three-foot gap is ideal. Don't pass at full speed but don't go so slowly that steering becomes difficult.

SOUND SIGNALS

- * One short blast = I am turning to the right
- * * Two short blasts = I am turning to the left
- * * * Three short blasts = I am going in reverse

You are unlikely to remember more than this in the heat of the moment! But navigation guides covering waters where you are likely to need this knowledge will have it included.

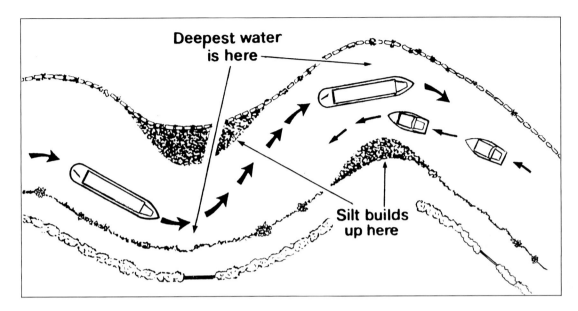

Deepest water
is here

Silt builds
up here

All rules have exceptions, though. You may meet a boat that is much larger than yours, and which needs the deeper water on the outside of a bend and will want you to pass on the right – the diagram above shows the situation. The helmsman may indicate this with a sound signal as he steers across from one side to the other, or he may just hold his course on the left side.

Sound signals are rarely used, and then usually on rivers. If you hear a frantic toot on a canal it generally means that someone has just seen you and is afraid you haven't seen them! But it's as well to be aware of what they mean, and if it's a working boat of any kind (and that includes pleasure steamers) then you need to listen, work out what it is telling you and act accordingly.

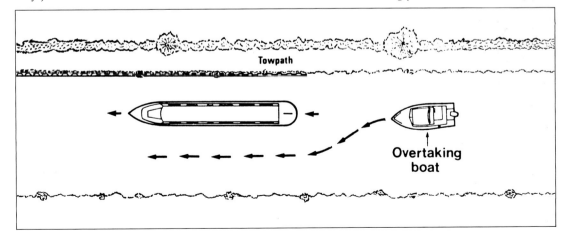

Towpath

Overtaking
boat

As a general rule the towpath side of the canal or river is the accepted mooring side. This does not mean that you will find the ideal mooring place just anywhere along the towpath – it may be overgrown, shallow, private or alongside a factory that works a night shift! You will often find mooring sites indicated by signboards, stating how long you can stay. Pub moorings are popular, so don't plan to arrive too late; if you have young children aboard, check the whereabouts of the pub car park, because there is always a lot of noise at closing time. The same goes for railways: check the map before you moor in that idyllic isolated spot – you could have inter-city trains on the other side of the hedge! *Don't* moor on a bend, close to bridges or locks, or in very narrow sections of canal.

Having chosen a likely spot, slow down and approach the bank with care. If there are mooring rings or posts you can be reasonably sure that the water is deep enough. A collapsed bank probably means that there is debris in the water below. If you can see weed under the surface the water may not necessarily be too shallow, but you are liable to foul the propeller.

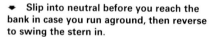

◆ If you are mooring a cruiser, attach the mooring rope to the cleat, then feed it through the fairlead and under the rail before coiling it ready to jump ashore.

◆ **Approach the mooring site slowly, with the bows at a gentle angle to the bank.**

◆ **Slip into neutral before you reach the bank in case you run aground, then reverse to swing the stern in.**

◆ **Be careful when you step ashore with a mooring rope: check that the ground is firm.**

MOORING TO A BOLLARD

➤ **Loop the mooring rope twice round the bollard to spread the strain.**

➤ **Take the free end over the part leading to the boat, and loop it through.**

➤ **Pull it tight and do it again: over, back under and through.**

➤ **Pull it tight. This knot is called a round turn and two half-hitches.**

Bows first is the rule during the approach. Point the boat at a gentle angle to the bank, and put the engine into neutral before you get there. Then if you do touch bottom the boat will stop before it pushes too far into the mud, and you'll find it easier to get off. If everything seems all right, put the engine into reverse and bring the stern in. Initially, you'll need someone standing by with a rope ready to hop off and hold the boat, but with a little practice you will soon be able to stop the boat just where you want to. Once you are proficient, there's no need to have the crew leaping to the bank and heaving away at ropes, trying to bring the boat to a standstill.

Take care when you do jump off the boat – the edge can be marshy or full of concealed potholes. It's best to wait until you are sure you can step onto firm ground.

➤ **Hold the bow and stern with the mooring ropes. The boat should be stationary.**

➤ **Knock the mooring pins into the bank with a club hammer. Smaller boats may be equipped with push-in mooring hooks.**

➤ **Tie each rope to the pin with a clove hitch and lead it back to the cleat on the boat.**

A lock is built to connect two different levels of water. On a river, a lock replaces a waterfall or a stretch of rapids, but canal engineers used locks to carry the canal up and over high ground. On a canal the stretch of water between each lock is called a 'pound' and may be any distance from a few yards to a number of miles. There are gates at each end of the lock to let boats in and out. In the gates are apertures called sluices, and these are sealed by paddles. When the paddles are lifted, using a windlass, water flows through the sluices, to empty or fill the lock. A boat can only go through the gates when the water level inside the lock is the same as that on which the boat is floating.

Whether you want to go up or down, you have to get your boat into the lock, then raise or lower the water level so that you can get out at the other end. You will need to pull into the bank or landing stage to put one of the crew ashore with the windlass to do the work. You may have to fill or empty the lock before you can get in if the water levels are not equal. Once the boat is in the lock, close the gates behind you and check that the paddles at that end are closed. Then you can move to the other end of the lock to operate the paddles there. When the water is level with the stretch you want to move into you will be able to open the gates and move your boat out of the lock.

◆ Tie up the boat, or it may be pulled into the gates by the current as the lock fills.

◆ If the lock is empty, open the paddles at the top of the lock to fill it. Engage the ratchets and remove the windlass.

◆ When the lock is full, open the top gates. Carefully wind the paddles down.

◆ Open both the lower paddles to empty the lock again.

◆ Control the boat as it falls by slipping the mooring ropes. Be sure someone is watching the boat all the time.

◆ When the water has stopped flowing out of the lock chamber, open the lower set of gates.

Paddle gear has often been doing its job for a long time, and needs to be handled carefully – or it may not be working for you next year! If you find it difficult to raise a paddle, turn the windlass just enough to let a little water through; when the pressure has eased off a bit, you'll find that the windlass will turn much easier. In any case, it is unwise to wind the paddles up too quickly if you are filling a lock. If you do you are likely to swamp a boat that has its bows close up to the lock gates, and the rush of water will set boats swinging in all directions. Where there are ground paddles, these should be operated first, using the same technique of opening them a short way first, not least because some of them have a nasty habit of shooting water upwards at the unsuspecting operator.

The windlass that is used to turn the paddle gear should *never* be left on the spindle. Operate the paddle, engage the ratchet and *remove the windlass*. Then if the ratchet slips or is knocked off, you won't have a lethal lump of metal catapulting through the air.

◆ **The sequence below shows the stages in going down a broad lock. Narrow locks are basically the same, but may have only one gate at each end. The sequence overleaf shows the stages in going up a lock.**

◆ **Take the boat into the lock chamber and stop at the far end, away from the sill.**

◆ **Close the upper set of gates.**

◆ **Make sure the boat is clear of the sill, and hold it with two lines passed round bollards.**

◆ **Motor out of the lock and stop, ready to pick up the crew.**

◆ **Close the lower gates.**

◆ **Lower the paddles in the bottom gates.**

● **Before going up a lock, stop to let off the crew!**

● **Check that the paddles in the lower gates are down.**

● **Open the lower gates.**

● **If the flow of water is fierce, control the boat in the lock with the mooring ropes.**

● **As the boat rises in the lock, open the other top paddle.**

● **When the water level inside and outside the lock is the same, open the top gates.**

It is vital to avoid wasting water when operating locks. The water supply to canals is limited by the storage capacity of the reservoirs which feed most canals.

Take a look at the situation shown opposite: the boat is going uphill and has come to a full lock. You can see that the lock must be emptied of water before the boat can get in, and filled again before it can leave at the top level. This means that two lockfuls of water are being used to get one boat through. The same would apply if the boat was going down and was faced with an empty lock.

If another boat was coming in the opposite direction it could come down as the lock emptied. So in this situation you should always look for oncoming boats – if the lock is sited on a bend, send one of the crew off to have a quick look round the corner ahead of you. You should always share locks with other boats whenever possible, making the most of every lockful of water, so look behind you too.

◆ Motor into the lock chamber.

◆ Shut the lower gates and check again that their paddles are closd, or the lock will not fill.

◆ Open one top paddle, on the side opposite the boat.

◆ Motor out of the lock.

◆ Lower the top paddles, taking care that they do not drop out of control.

◆ Close the top gates, and continue on your way.

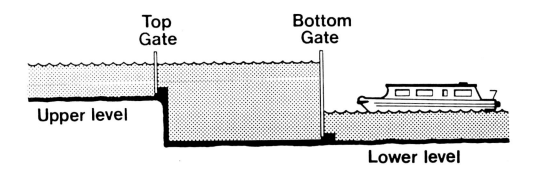

Top Gate

Bottom Gate

Upper level

Lower level

Many river navigations (and commercial water-ways) have locks that are manned at set times during the day – for example from eight or nine in the morning until dusk. The times vary throughout the year. The lock-keeper will work the lock for boats to go through and may also be responsible for the control of water levels in his stretch of the river. Where a lock is manned you must obey the lock-keeper's instructions.

When you approach a manned lock and the gates are closed, you should wait at the landing stage if possible, or pull in towards the side so that you are not in the way of craft coming out of the lock. If there are lots of other boats around, remember that they are waiting too. Don't go steaming straight up to the lock gates; this causes extreme irritation to those waiting and chaos when the gates open and you are in the way! If there is a space on the landing stage, pull up as close as you can to the boat in front so that as many boats as possible can squeeze in.

➡ **Control the position of the boat in the lock using the mooring rope – slipping it slowly as the boat falls, or taking up slack as it rises.**

Once you are inside the lock, the lock-keeper may take your rope, which he will pass round a bollard and return to you; or you may have to get off the boat and do the job yourself. In some locks you hold on to chains or ropes hanging from the lock walls. Whatever happens, do not tie the boat up fast – the rope must be free to run while you hold the other end and control the boat as it rises or falls with the water level.

If you're faced with throwing the rope up to the lock keeper, try not to rush it. Coil the rope properly, and throw it underarm. This is something well worth practising on a quiet bit of mooring – it's not difficult, but it takes a little time to get the hang of, especially coiling the rope in the first place (this is why you should always leave ropes neatly coiled after use).

Once you are safely in the lock with several other boats the lock-keeper will shut the gates and open the paddles. Going down is usually a gentle procedure but when a lock is filling the rush of water may tend to push your bows away from the lockside. Don't wait until this happens and then begin a tug-of-war with your boat. Keep the ropes held firm without straining on them and you'll find it quite easy. There's a lot to watch: the bows, the stern (to make sure you don't run back onto the boat behind) and the side (to see that you don't wedge other boats).

You may find that the lock-keeper will ask you to turn off your engine if you have not already done so. This is not just officialdom asserting itself; it's because, in the event of any mishap, you would not be able to hear his instructions above the engine noise. This can also apply to loud radios on deck.

Coming out of the lock you should keep your speed down because you may be passing very close to moored boats waiting to go in.

On rivers the water diverted from the lock flows over a weir. This can be a hazard, and after heavy rain the 'pull' of the water flowing over the weir is considerable; when going down-stream keep well over to the opposite bank.

BRIDGES

Approach bridges with caution: early canal builders seemed to delight in siting narrow bridges on bends, making it difficult to see boats coming in the opposite direction. Don't be afraid to sound your horn, and it helps to have someone keeping a look-out on the bows. If there is another boat in view, the boat nearest the bridge has right of way, but if you're in a small craft it's courteous – and safer – to let a bigger boat through first. This is because a small boat is generally more manoeuvrable and better able to wait in shallow water. Don't try making a race of it; if there is any doubt about your precedence pull into the side and indicate clearly if you want the other boat to come through.

Narrow canal bridges do sometimes look as if the boat will be a tight fit, but you will get through! Just take it steady, keep over to the towpath side and don't reduce speed to such an extent that steering becomes difficult. Watch the height, too. Some bridges have very restricted headroom so make sure anyone sitting on the roof has seen the bridge coming – and gets off in time!

← Each canal bridge has a number. You'll find the number in the navigation guide, and in most cases it is displayed on the bridge itself, as here.

COILING AND THROWING A ROPE

← Measure out a length of rope for coiling by holding your arms apart, running it though your right hand.

← Bring your hands together to add the length to the coil, twisting it clockwise to prevent it kinking.

← When you've coiled the whole rope, split the coil into two halves, one in each hand, ready for throwing.

← Throw the free coil underarm so that it uncoils in the air, and pay out more rope from the other half as required.

The canal builders had as many difficulties planning the route as the motorway builders of today. Many objections came from farmers whose fields were to be divided by the new waterways, and these were overcome by putting in movable bridges. Lifting bridges gave access for cattle from field to field, and the larger swing bridges were able to accommodate farm carts and other vehicles.

The majority of these bridges now carry very little traffic and many are left open permanently or, sadly, have been taken away. Occasionally you will find one that is still open to road traffic; somehow these always seem to be the slowest to operate and you must be prepared to find a queue of cars building up and impatiently watching you do the hard work. Obviously under these circumstances you try to get through as quickly as possible. If there is no barrier to put down against traffic, make sure that any oncoming vehicles are aware of what's going on – and don't forget to close the bridge behind you.

The simplest bridges to operate are the counterbalanced lifting bridges, as found on the Oxford Canal; the bridge is counterbalanced by beams and a chain hanging from the beam gives you something to heave on and raise the bridge. Once the bridge is lifted you must make sure that it stays that way – there may be a fixing provided or you can sit on the beam itself, but don't just assume that it will stay down. *Never* allow children to handle these bridges by themselves. They will not always be able (or remember) to hold the bridge and there's a real danger of it coming back down on your boat. There are more sophisticated lifting bridges that need a windlass to operate the lifting mechanism.

Swing bridges also come in a variety of designs: from straightforward push-across jobs to some rather odd ones with complicated arrangements of gears and wheels. These will have operating instructions posted on a panel alongside.

Whatever type of bridge you encounter, you'll need to put someone ashore to operate the mechanism – a fairly hefty crew member is usually a good idea! And do leave the bridge as you found it, after checking that there isn't another boat in sight. If you leave the bridge open for another boat, be sure that they understand the need to close it after passing through.

◆ **This lifting bridge on the Stratford Canal has counterweighted beams to hold it open.**

↩ **Swing bridges are more trouble, but safer. Keep well away from all movable bridges until they are open.**

TUNNELS

The first requirement for navigating in tunnels is a good headlight, which you can adjust to any angle. A hand-held torch just will not do. If your route includes long tunnels, make sure that the boat's battery is well charged, because the headlight uses a lot of power. Lengths of tunnels are given in navigation guides and at tunnel entrances.

A few tunnels are not wide enough for two boats to pass, in which case there will either be a tunnel-keeper to organise things or a system whereby boats are allowed each way at certain times; the timetable is always displayed at the tunnel entrance. (It is assumed that your boat is of no more than seven-foot beam; if it is wider than this you should contact the relevant British Waterways office who will advise you – see address list.)

If you are in a tunnel and you see a boat coming towards you, ease over to the right-hand side and make sure your spotlight is directed at the wall well ahead of you – not straight into the other steerer's eyes! Don't slow down too much or you may have difficulty steering. If both craft are steel-hulled narrowboats don't panic if you do bump sides with the other boat; you won't do much harm, though the sound echoing through the tunnel will seem horrendous. But if you are steering a narrowboat and you are passing a small cruiser, remember that any bump is the equivalent of a double-decker bus colliding with a Mini, so keep clear! You should always treat smaller boats with care and courtesy, wherever you are.

Tunnels can often be wet: the ventilation shafts admit water as well as fresh air! This may

♦ **You will need a powerful headlight to negotiate tunnels. Check that yours is in good working order, and ensure that the boat's battery is well charged.**

consist of just a few drops or amount to a downpour, so it's as well to put all radios, books, cameras and what-have-you inside the cabin before going into the tunnel. But if you're in a cruiser, don't be tempted to put the cockpit cover up, as this will only impede your view and could be awkward in tunnels with restricted headroom.

Children should always view tunnels from the inside of the boat; the engine noise is magnified to such an extent that splashes or cries for help are quite inaudible. You have enough to do without counting heads every few minutes!

Note that unpowered craft are not allowed in some tunnels. This is indicated in the navigation guide and at the tunnel entrance. You may also see a height gauge at the entrance. This won't bother you if you have an average boat, but if you are in something with added height, don't be tempted to lift the gauge and squeeze under – the gauge does represent the absolute maximum height.

For those who feel they can't face a long underground journey, there is nearly always a path over the top of the hill, especially where there is no towpath inside the tunnel.

Canal holidays aren't really fraught with danger! It's just that everyone's favourite holiday tales tend to grow in the telling, like the fisherman's 'one that got away'. There are some hazards, however, and even the most experienced navigators don't avoid them all.

Floating debris

Debris in the water is one of the most common problems; in some areas people seem to regard the canal as their local rubbish tip. Large items of furniture have been encountered, but this is a fairly infrequent occurrence!

The polythene bag is a well known offender – it can wrap itself around your propeller and stop it dead. The only solution is to stop the engine, get at the propeller and untwist or cut off the polythene. Weed will also entwine itself around the prop., not necessarily stopping it, but often causing a noticeable loss of speed. Giving the engine a sharp burst in reverse will often be sufficient to throw off the weed.

Getting caught on the sill of a lock

This can be disastrous and is almost always the result of carelessness. If you are going down in a lock the problem may arise as the water level falls and the stern of the boat catches on the sill – a sort of 'doorstep' at the foot of the top gate. If you have allowed your boat to drift too far back the stern will ground itself on the sill while the bow will keep going down with the water. If this happens close the paddles at once, then refill the lock until the boat is floating again. This sounds easy, but closing paddles when the water is rushing through them is difficult, and it is much better to avoid the situation.

A similar problem can arise (although with cruisers rather than narrowboats) if the boat gets caught on projections or uneven masonry on the walls of the lock. Your boat can also get wedged with another boat, or get its fend-offs caught up; you can also tie your boat up too tightly before dashing off to empty the lock – with spectacular results! Locks are ideal places for meeting other

USING THE WEED HATCH

✦ If the propeller of a narrowboat becomes choked with weed, you can clear it through the weed hatch. Stop the engine and unclamp the metal bar that secures the lid.

✦ Once the bar is removed you can lift the lid to reveal a slot in the bottom of the hull directly above the propeller. You should be able to see the problem.

✦ Reach down into the water to clear the obstruction – and don't drop it back in the canal near the propeller! Then replace the lid and securing bar, and clamp them up tightly.

boats and chatting, but you must *always* keep a close watch on your own boat.

Going aground

This happens to everyone sooner or later, although with care it shouldn't happen too often. Take the engine out of gear as soon as you touch bottom, and if the bows have grounded but the stern is still afloat you should be able to reverse off quite easily. Make sure that the crew move away from the end – or side – of the boat that is aground. This in itself may be sufficient to float you off, and a gentle rocking of the boat may help too. Pushing off with the boathook may help – although doing this may well swing the floating end of the boat around to join the grounded end.

It's best to avoid going aground in the first place. Remember that silt builds up on the inside of bends, so when you are going round a bend stick to the middle, and don't be tempted to cut corners.

Fishermen

Slow down when you pass anglers and keep away from the bank. It may appear that you are going to run into the rod – but it will be whisked away before you get too close!

Can I swim?

Never swim in canals. It's not allowed and it's not safe – you could injure yourself on underwater obstructions or get caught up in weeds.

On rivers, particularly the Thames, there are places that are obviously well used by the local people for a dip in hot weather. But remember that the water may be very deep in the centre of the river and that there may be odd currents or other peculiarities known to the locals, but not to you. If you want a swim it is far better to find the nearest swimming bath.

☛ **If you use the pole to push off, use it above the water level or you may pierce the clay lining of the canal. Stand on the opposite side of the boat to help rock it off the bank.**

The familiar working boats or narrowboats are of the same basic shape as the boats used in the Duke of Bridgewater's underground mines, because the first locks were built to accommodate these boats, and subsequent boats were built to fit the locks. It's no accident that a narrowboat fits exactly into a narrow lock! The boats were up to 70 feet in length, with a beam of not more than seven feet. Their box-like hulls were slab-sided and were originally constructed of wood. Later boats were built of iron and wood, and finally all-steel hulls became the norm.

Today's narrowboats come in all sizes, from around 25 feet up to 70 feet, but all have the vital beam dimension of 6ft 10in. They are still the most popular type of boat for canal cruising. There are plenty of small cruisers suitable for use on inland waters, though, and many of these have the added advantage that it is possible to trail them, giving access to waterways far from the home base and to waterways that are not connected to the main system.

Whatever type of boat you buy, don't be tempted to go wider than 6ft 10in if your main interest is canal cruising. A glance at the map will demonstrate the frustration of owning a boat wider than this: narrow connecting canals will make some routes inaccessible, the narrow Northampton Arm from the Grand Union to the Nene being a prime example. The length is also a consideration – a 70-foot boat, for example, will be too long for the Leeds and Liverpool, where the locks are around 60 feet long, and it is not possible to explore the Middle Level in a boat that is more than 49 feet long.

Generally if your beam and length are appropriate, then draft and headroom shouldn't be a problem. For general guidance, a boat drawing less than 2ft 6in should be able to navigate all waterways without any trouble. If you have a boat with a draught greater than this you should check first: the maximum dimensions are given in the navigation guides, but if in doubt consult

➥ **Cruising narrowboats are the most popular craft for long trips on the canals: they have good accommodation and are tailor-made for the system. A small cruiser is better for short trips, and has the advantage that it can be trailed behind a car.**

the navigation authority. For unrestricted navigation the height of the boat should not be more than six feet above water level, though for carefree boating a little less is desirable.

Narrowboats can be bought in all stages of construction – from a bare hull and cabin top to a complete boat fitted out to your own design. Finishing a boat from a bare hull is a formidable task, but those who are prepared to tackle this will make considerable savings on cost.

So the choice of boat is wide – and so is the price range! New and secondhand boats are advertised in boating and waterway magazines, and these advertisements will give you some idea of the current price range. The finance for your purchase can be arranged in various ways: banks and building societies will have schemes available, and there are specialist companies offering loans for boat purchase.

◗ **Large cruisers are luxurious, but often restricted to waterways with broad locks.**

➠ **A restored working boat has limited accommodation, but immense appeal for the canal enthusiast.**

Either you're a technical wizard – or you're not! Those who can reduce a car to a heap of parts and re-assemble it without any trouble will find the diesel engine that is installed in most narrowboats quite straightforward. Assessing the condition of the engine in a secondhand boat or choosing the engine for a new one should prove a simple matter.

If you are not in this happy position, what do you do? If you are buying a complete new boat from a reputable builder, take his advice – he will know which type of engine suits his boat best, and advise on the options.

When you are buying secondhand the engine installed will be the previous owner's choice, not yours. You will obviously go for a trial run and note whether the engine appears to run smoothly, but you should also have a look at the installation. Is the engine easily accessible for daily checks and maintenance? Are the controls (the throttle and gearshift, which may be combined in a single lever) easily accessible from the

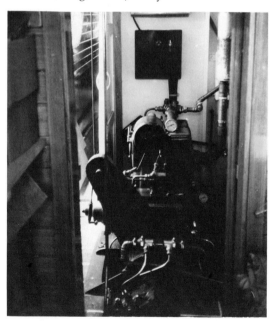

steering position? How noisy is the engine? Inboard engines can be noisy and if the engine is badly installed you may find it difficult to hold a conversation with the person next to you when you're steering! This is an extreme case, but it's well worth wandering through the boat while underway to check on the noise levels.

Bearing in mind the fact that the speed limit on canals is restricted to four miles an hour, you don't need an engine that will move your boat much faster than this. But if you intend to cruise on rivers or tidal waters you will need some spare power in hand, so bear this in mind when you are asking the questions. A cruiser – especially a trailed boat – will probably be used on a wide range of waters and may well be powered by an outboard motor. The huge motors that can take you around the coast in a cloud of spray are far too big for canals – and they won't take kindly to being run at slow speed. For canal use you should avoid anything over 20hp, but since outboards are simple to change you could always keep a low-power motor for inland use only.

You may also be faced with the choice between a petrol or diesel engine. Petrol engines are cheaper to buy initially, but a diesel uses much less fuel and also scores on safety grounds.

There are two other options, not so readily available, but becoming more popular all the time; these are steam engines and electric motors. There are some delightful steam launches being built for those lazy summer afternoons on the river, but they are somewhat expensive. The Steam Boat Association is a useful contact if this is where your interest lies. The Electric Boat Association will also give you information; electric boats are wonderfully quiet but they need their batteries charging fairly frequently and the number of places where this can be done afloat is, as yet, limited.

◀ **Make sure that you can get at the engine for routine maintenance. This is a narrowboat installation.**

FITTING OUT

Apart from obvious things such as the engine, cooker, mattresses and so on, you will need to think about all the extra equipment which may or may not be included in the purchase price of a new or secondhand boat, and will certainly have to be taken into account if you are building your own boat.

Ropes are essential. You will need at least one stern and one bow line, each at least 30 feet (nine metres) long. If you are going to cruise the larger river navigations 50 feet (15 metres) is a better length. You will need **mooring pins** of a suitable size for the boat; narrowboats use hefty spikes and a hammer, but if you have a small cruiser you can get away with a lighter 'push-in' type. River users need at least one **anchor**, complete with a good length of chain, and this should be kept ready for immediate use.

Fire extinguishers are sensible and specifically required by most navigation authorities. They should be sited to cover cooking areas, the engine, any sources of heating and all exits from the boat.

Navigation lights aren't normally found in narrowboats. Hired boats are not allowed to navigate after dark, and private boats are advised not to do so. Nevertheless you must have a good white **spotlight** for tunnels. Cruisers are usually equipped with port and starboard lights; some river navigations stipulate stern and masthead lights as well.

An electrically-operated **horn** or the hand-held aerosol variety is a necessity.

For canal cruising you will need a selection of **windlasses** for working locks and bridges. Always carry spares – they often fall into the water or get left behind at locks!

Make sure you've got a **boathook**, at least one, of an appropriate size for the boat. You will need a **deck mop** too, if your deck is larger than a plastic sponge can cope with.

♦ **A fire can rapidly destroy a boat, so make sure you have enough fire extinguishers of the right type.**

You may need an extra **petrol tank** if you have an outboard engine, and additional **water containers**, as well as a length of **hose** to fill the large built-in water tank.

Cruisers need **fend-offs** all round; narrowboats use traditional rope fenders at bow and stern.

These are mainly external extras. Inside, the fitting out becomes a matter of personal choice, but unless you are going to carry large quantities of equipment back and forth to the boat each weekend you will need to double up on all domestic essentials such as saucepans, cutlery and crockery.

You should also note that some of the items mentioned are required by various bylaws and the regulations imposed by navigation authorities. There are also quite strict rules about gas and electrical installations; newly-built boats will almost certainly comply with these standards, but if you're buying secondhand you need to check that everything is in order.

Your boat must be licensed or registered on nearly all waterways. The navigation guides list the relevant authorities. The charges are based on the size of the boat, and most authorities issue licences for periods ranging from one week to one year. In some cases these can be arranged 'on the spot' but it's advisable to make arrangements well in advance of your holiday whenever possible.

Incidentally, canoes, sailing dinghies, rowing boats and inflatables also need licences, although these cost less than for powered boats. The British Waterways Board has a special arrangement for members of the British Canoe Union.

Boats used for residential purposes need a special licence. The issue of these is limited and is often subject to approval of the mooring, so if you're thinking about living afloat, you need to make sure that you can find a suitable site for your boat.

Moorings

Finding a permanent mooring can be a problem or it can be easy – it all depends on what sort of

◆ **Bray Marina on the Thames is typical of the many well-equipped marinas to be found today on inland waters.**

mooring you want. Would you feel happy with a cheaper bankside mooring, with maybe a long walk from the road , or do you want full marina services? Have you got time to undertake a fairly long drive from home before you can start cruising, or has your mooring got to be on the nearest accessible stretch of waterway?

The number of marinas on inland waters is increasing. These offer secure moorings and most will have water, fuel and chandlery available plus toilets and rubbish disposal points. Many also have shower facilities. Boatyards will probably offer many of these services, and there's usually someone who can deal with repairs and maintenance. Boat clubs usually have moorings for members, though you may find a waiting list in some areas. British Waterways have some bankside moorings available and will supply a list of these, as will other navigation authorities.

You can expect to pay more for marina and boatyard moorings. The charges are usually per foot, per week – so maybe you don't want to own a 70-footer after all! Indeed, before committing yourself to buying a boat, you need to make sure you've got somewhere to keep it; mooring charges can be a significant part of a boat's running costs, so they are worth investigating at an early stage.

Marinas and boatyards advertise in boating magazines, which will also have 'moorings' sections in their small ads. The ultimate luxury is a waterside house with its own mooring – these are also advertised in the waterway magazines! On a more practical level, you may find that non-boating owners of such properties offer to let their moorings, and these opportunities are also advertised in the back pages of the boating press.

Trailing
Trailing is an alternative to keeping a boat permanently on a mooring, and has several advantages. You can save on mooring fees – provided you have adequate garden space to accommodate your boat (it may look small in the water, but it will grow to huge proportions when you are trying to hide it behind the rose bushes in the front garden). Some boatyards and marinas will offer on-shore storage, which will be a little cheaper than a mooring. But the major benefit associated with trailing is that you have the entire waterway system to play with! You can get

your boat to isolated waterways – there's the Lancaster Canal, the Brecon and Abergavenney Canal, the Scottish canals, the Broads and the Lake District. You also have the option of coastal and estuary cruising, provided that your boat and engine are suitable.

Disadvantages? The size of your boat will be restricted to around 24 to 27 feet, depending on its weight, and you obviously need a suitable car with a towing hitch (a 1600cc family saloon will cope with a 17-foot fibreglass cruiser). And although the freedom of choice for a fortnight's holiday is a great asset, launching and retrieving the boat for just a brief weekend will take up a lot of precious cruising time.

There are plenty of suitable boats on the market. Several are specially built for trailing and inland cruising, with plenty of space inside, standing headroom and the capability of sleeping up to four people.

Boat builders will advise on suitable trailers for their boats, and may supply both together as a complete package. There are very detailed regulations regarding trailing; if you buy a package, then your supplier will advise, as will trailer manufacturers and the motoring organisations.

➡ **If you can trail your boat, you can penetrate every corner of the waterways network. This small canal boat is specially designed for trailing, and can be launched wherever there is a slipway.**

Wherever you go on the waterways you will find a lot to look at. The villages and towns along the route have their own interest, and the waterside wildlife is a continual joy, but for many enthusiasts it is the engineering of the waterways themselves that is the main attraction.

Bridges come in all shapes and sizes, though each waterway tends to have style of its own: red-brick bridges on the Oxford Canal, split bridges on the Stratford Canal (the gap was for the tow-rope to pass through) and offset bridges on the Leeds and Liverpool Canal, with the centres helpfully marked. More recent structures are also of interest – the spans carrying the motorways over the canals in Birmingham give the navigator a unique view of Spaghetti Junction from below!

◆ **Cast-iron elegance: a masterpiece of nineteenth-century engineering on the Grand Union Canal.**

Look out for turnover bridges, built where the towpath crosses the canal. These were designed so that the towing horse could change sides without unhitching the rope from the boat: the towpath ascends a ramp, crosses the bridge and spirals down under the arch. There's a good example at Marple, where the Peak Forest Canal and Macclesfield Canal meet. Watch for the variety of movable bridges: some lifting vertically and some swinging horizontally.

These different types of bridge are all interesting and usually pleasing on the eye – the more so because in general the simple and often very elegant designs are purely functional rather than self-consciously decorative.

Locks look much alike at first – they all have gates, balance beams and paddle gear – but the variations are infinite. The balance beams may be made of timber or steel, and old telegraph poles have been used in some places. Some locks

have long, square-section wooden beams, which are good and solid, nice to push against when opening the gate and excellent for resting on when the weather is warm! Where alterations to the original surroundings of the lock have reduced the space available, short cranked beams are often installed; these lack the visual attraction of the standard black-and-white painted variety and are also very awkward to push against. Lock gates are usually built of timber, although a few steel ones were installed – you can see some examples of these on the Oxford Canal.

Tunnels are not very spectacular from outside, but as you move inside the blackness seems to leap at you – and you wonder if the spotlight is really working! You might think that there isn't much to see in a tunnel anyway, but once you become adjusted to the darkness you will start to notice things. Look for the ventilation shafts set at intervals in the longer tunnels – and don't forget that these are liable to shower you with water! These shafts can be seen above ground too, and you can follow the route of the tunnel if you're walking over the top.

Inside the tunnel there will be distance markers to tell you how far you've gone. Worn patches on the walls mark the passage of generations of boats, some of which might have been 'legged' through the tunnel. 'Legging' was one of the odder occupations connected with canals. In the days of horse traction there was no way of towing a boat through a tunnel without a towpath. Two men, one on each side, lay at the bows of the boat and 'walked' along the tunnel walls to push the boat through, while the horse was taken over the top of the hill. Legging was an exhausting job and the leggers must have watched the distance markers keenly, for some tunnels are over two miles long.

♦ **Not all tunnels are long, dark and dank. Cowley Tunnel on the Shropshire Union is little more than a bridge of rock over the canal.**

◄ **Nantwich Aqueduct – a cast-iron trough carrying the Shropshire Union Canal over a minor road.**

In the eighteenth century it was proposed that the Bridgewater Canal should be carried over the River Irwell by means of an **aqueduct**. If people, horses and carts could cross rivers by bridges, why not extend this to water and boats? At that time, local opinion thought the whole idea ridiculous and referred to the scheme as a 'castle in the air', but the engineers knew what they were doing. Barton Aqueduct was built as planned, and survived until the end of the nineteenth century when it was replaced by the present aqueduct – a massive structure which swings aside to allow the passage of vessels on the Manchester Ship Canal.

More aqueducts followed Barton. The first were of brick or stone, but later structures incorporated cast iron. Many splendid examples still remain, including Pontcysyllte on the Llangollen Canal, Marple on the Peak Forest Canal, the Lune Aqueduct on the Lancaster Canal, and Dundas and Avoncliffe on the Kennet and Avon. Some are high but of no great length; unless you check in your navigation guide, you may not even realise you've crossed one! If you are cruising it's a good idea to leave the boat and have a look at an aqueduct from the nearest convenient vantage point since the view from the boat is restricted to a long narrow strip of water.

There are many smaller details worth looking out for: number plates and name plates on locks and bridges; signs telling you how far it is to the next lock, or how far you are from the nearest major canal junction. Some of these signs carry the initials of the original canal companies – on the Grand Union you'll see mile posts with the letter GJCC on them, a legacy of the days when the Grand Union was run by the Grand Junction Canal Company.

Sadly, many of these interesting features are disappearing. Old bridges have been replaced by new; warehouses and other canalside buildings have given way to modern structures; lock cottages that are no longer lived in have become derelict. But much is also being restored, and in many places old buildings have been put to new uses. For example, canalside warehouses at Ellesmere Port in Cheshire and Gloucester Docks in the south-west of the network have been transformed into excellent waterway museums and many smaller buildings around the system are used as visitor centres, water activity centres, craft workshops or as sites for local history exhibitions.

The navigation guides will list many of the interesting things to be seen – it's up to you to spot the rest!

Towpath Walking
For those who enjoy walking, canal towpaths have a lot to offer. When first built they were good, flat wide paths alongside every waterway made for the horses which towed the boats before the steam engine was available. The horses were efficient and popular: for many years after the first steam engines were installed in canal boats some boatmen preferred real horsepower to its mechanical replacement.

⬧ **Canal engineering at its finest: Pontcysyllte Aqueduct on the Llangollen Canal.**

⬧ **New developments such as the revamped Gas Street Basin in Birmingham are changing the face of the canals.**

With the general disappearance of the plodding canal horse the towpath has become narrowed down and in some places it has become difficult to follow. But don't let this deter you – an Ordnance Survey map will show you alternative routes if the path is totally impassable and the navigation guides will also indicate the problem sections and ways round them.

You'll be walking at the same speed as a boat, and it will take you less time to go by a lock, so in a day you will get further on your feet than you would in a boat. You will also probably see more, as you can stop to take a closer look at waterside wildlife or divert to investigate the canalside villages.

Walking also gives you the opportunity to explore derelict canals and routes that are being restored but are not yet open for navigation. Tracing the route of a long-disused canal often involves a fair bit of detective work. Ordnance Survey maps help; Imray's map of the British waterways shows the location of disused canals, and there are a number of books on towpath walking available.

If this book has sparked your interest in canal and river cruising you will want to know how to get more specific information about particular waterways or boats.

At the end of this section you will find some useful addresses. The Inland Waterways Association's General Office will always be pleased to help, and if you want to meet other people with an interest in waterways, or if you would like to support the work going on to improve the canal system, then you should consider joining the Association yourself. There are more than 35 branches throughout the country, and they all hold regular meetings, stage summer events and visit canals in other areas. There may also be a canal society near you which takes an interest in one particular canal, usually with restoration as its main object.

The IWA has a wide range of books available covering every aspect of canals, including navigation guides, canal history, narrowboats and towpath walking.

For a general view of the waterway system, there are at least two maps available. The Waterways World series of guides to individual canals are excellent; they cover many popular routes, but not the entire system. The same can be said of the 'Canal Companions' series, which includes both single canals and ring routes. The guides published by Nicholsons in association with the Ordnance Survey cover most of the system, in seven sections, including the River Thames.

There are magazines too. Waterways World, Canal Boat and Inland Waterways, and Canal and River Boat are monthly magazines dealing solely with inland waterways; they carry advertising for holiday hire, new and secondhand boats, and waterway events.

For information about boat licences, moorings and boat construction regulations you need to consult the relevant navigation authority. British Waterways controls a large part of the main canal network and the Scottish canals. Waterways that are not managed by BW include the River Thames (The Environment Agency for the non-tidal section above Teddington), the River Wey (National Trust), and the Warwickshire River Avon (Upper and Lower Avon Navigation Trusts). The addresses of all these authorities are included in the list. Details of other independent authorities are given in the appropriate navigation guides.

During the summer months IWA branches, canal societies and other water-related bodies hold events on the waterways. These range from small club gatherings to the IWA's annual National Festival, which is held at a different site each year, normally over the August Bank Holiday weekend. It features a large trade show where exhibitors include boat builders, hire companies, engine manufacturers, canal societies and craft exhibitors. There's also a rally of boats, attracting some 500 entries of all types from canoes to ex-working narrowboats, lovingly restored by their owners. Waterway theatre groups also perform during the weekend. This is definitely the ideal place to find out more, all on one site!

You can also visit the major boat shows. There's the London show held at Earls Court in January; and the Southampton show in September. Neither of these are particularly 'inland' orientated, but both have IWA stands. The major holiday booking agencies have stands at Earls Court and although you are unlikely to see many narrowboats you will find several manufacturers of cruisers and engines suitable for inland use as well as a wide variety of chandlery and clothing stands. A smaller show, but with more narrowboats on view, is held at Birmingham's National Exhibition Centre in February.

If you want a day out you can visit one of the museums which are totally devoted to canals or which have a strong waterways link. You'll also find many smaller museums around the canal system, some using old waterside buildings.

USEFUL ADDRESSES

For general information on waterways and a list of waterway books for sale, contact:

> The Inland Waterways Association
> 114 Regent's Park Road
> London NW1 8UQ

IWA will also send you details of membership of the Association and can put you in touch with your local branch.

For general enquiries to British Waterways, information booklets, and licences and moorings on most (but not all) of the connecting canals in England and Wales, and the Scottish canals, you should contact:

> British Waterways
> Willow Grange
> Church Road
> Watford WD1 3QA

Boat hire – central booking agencies

> Hoseasons Boating Holidays
> Sunway House
> Lowestoft
> Suffolk NR32 3LT

> Blakes Holidays
> Wroxham
> Norfolk NR12 8DH

> The Association of Pleasure Craft Operators
> 35a High Street
> Newport
> Shropshire TF10 8JW

The list below is a selection of the most popular waterways that are not managed by BW. There are others; the IWA will be able to identify which Authority you need and provide addresses.

River Thames (above Teddington)

> The Environment Agency
> Thames Region
> PO Box 214
> Reading
> RG1 8HQ

River Whey

> The National Trust
> Dapdune Lea
> Wharf Road
> Guildford
> Surrey

River Avon, upper reaches (above Evesham)

> The Upper Avon Navigation Trust
> Avon House
> Harvington
> Evesham
> Worcestershire WR11 5NR

River Avon, lower reaches (below Evesham)

> The Lower Avon Navigation Trust
> Holloway
> Pershore
> Worcestershire WR10 1HW

Norfolk Broads

> The Broads Authority
> Thomas Harvey House
> 18 Colegate
> Norwich
> Norfolk NR3 1BQ

Air draft The height of the boat above water level.

Barge General term for wide-beam working boats on inland waterways. This does not include traditional working boats.

Beam The width of the boat.

Bollard Short mooring post found at locks and 'official' mooring places.

Bows The front of the boat.

Buckby can The brightly-painted water can that forms part of the equipment of a traditional narrowboat; usually accompanied by a bowl resembling a truncated bucket.

Butty Narrowboats originally worked in pairs, with a powered boat – the motor – towing a non-powered boat known as the butty. The narrowboat crew lived in the small back cabin of the motor, and the rest of the boat was devoted to cargo space.

Canal A completely artificial waterway.

Cut Another word for canal, but usually referring to a short canal that bypasses a tortuous or unnavigable stretch of river.

Draft The depth of the boat beneath water level. It is essential that you know this, since many canals are restricted in depth.

Feeder A channel carrying water to the upper levels of a canal.

Flight A series of locks very close together.

Ground paddle A sluice in the side of a lock instead of in the gate.

Guillotine gate A lock gate that is lifted to allow boats to pass beneath.

Headroom *see* Air draft.

Lock-wheeling The practice of sending one or more crew members along the towpath ahead of the boat to get the lock ready.

Motor *see* Butty.

Narrowboat The seven-foot beam boats which originaly worked the Midlands canals.

Navigation The old name for a canal. The labourers who built the navigations were called navigators, or navvies.

Paddle The sluice which has to be raised (drawn) to allow water in or out of a lock.

Port The left-hand side of the boat, as seen when facing forward. This term is not used on narrowboats.

Pound Any stretch of water between locks.

Reservoir The water store used to replenish the upper levels of the canal, replacing water that has drained away through the locks. Drought conditions reduce the amount of water stored in the reservoirs, and can cause the level of the canal to fall too low for navigation.

River navigation A river that has been dredged, straightened and provided with locks, so that boats can use it.

Side pond A small reservoir built alongside a lock, and designed to save water. The side pond has to be filled or emptied when using the lock; instructions are provided where they occur.

Sill The 'doorstep' at the foot of an upper lock gate. You must keep clear of the sill when the lock is emptying.

Staircase locks A series of locks that are so closely spaced that the bottom gates of one serve as the top gates of another.

Starboard The right-hand side of the boat as seen when facing forward. This term is not used on narrowboats.

Stern The back of the boat.

Stop lock Situated at the junction of canals owned by different companies, a stop lock was used to incarcerate a boat until the appropriate toll was paid. This system no longer operates!

Summit level The highest point of the canal.

Tidal lock A lock that separates the lower, tidal reaches of a navigable river from the upper, non-tidal reaches.

Windlass The cranked handle used to wind the paddles of locks up and down.